Cape Cod Visitor's Guide

Free and Inexpensive Things
To See and Do
In The
Mid-Cape Area

Dennis, Yarmouth, Hyannis

William E. Peace

Cape Cod Visitor's Guide
Free And Inexpensive Things To See And Do
In The Mid Cape Area
Dennis, Yarmouth, Hyannis

ISBN-13: 978-1511706483

ISBN-10: 1511706481

Printed in the United States of America

Preface

Cape Cod, a tiny peninsula jutting out into the Atlantic, the "Outermost of Lands," as Henry Beston had called it, attracts over 5 million visitors a year. On a summer day, more than 125,000 vehicles cross the Sagamore and Bourne Bridges that span the gorgeous 7-mile Cape Cod Canal, and with that symbolic crossing, visitors often leave all their worries behind.

White-sand beaches, cranberry bogs, dunes, lighthouses, bike paths, gentle ocean breezes and plenty of sun are all here for all to enjoy, and easy to find! But there are so many hidden gems on Cape Cod, not exactly secret places, but places a little off-the-beaten path, that many visitors miss out on some of the best things to see and do on the Cape. And so many of them are free or very inexpensive!

And that is exactly why this book is written. It is written from an "insider's" view, by a local resident who knows all the ins and outs of Cape Cod, all the back roads, and all the things to see, with the intent of sharing some of these wonderful locations for more to enjoy. It is written with everyone in mind, from the children to the adults in the family! This book focuses just on the Mid-Cape. From Scargo Tower to the Kennedy Memorial, from the Judah Baker Windmill to Bass Hole Boardwalk, Hyannis Harbor or Hokum Rock — there are many, many things to see and lots of "I didn't know that's" in Dennis, Yarmouth, and Hyannis.

Take a little time during your vacation to see just two or three spots each day, maybe after the beach, or on a rainy day, and you are certain to reflect wistfully when you do cross back over that Canal. Each place that you visit will make you want to stay on Cape Cod even longer! Enjoy your vacation! Leave the "mainland" behind!

S cargo Tower is a 28-foot stone tower perched atop Scargo Hill, which at 160 feet itself, is one of the highest hills on Cape Cod and the highest in the Midcape. It offers spectacular 360-degree views. The tower is free and open to the public during daylight hours and is definitely not to be missed. There is free parking for a small number of vehicles. While the views from the parking area itself are amazing, a narrow spiral metal staircase  provides access to the observation area at the top of the tower with even better views there. Due to the steep stairs and height of the structure itself, children do need to be watched carefully at Scargo Tower.

From the observation area, you can view nearly the entire Cape. Scargo is a favorite place for locals to view the sun setting over Cape Cod Bay, or fall foliage colors, although it can be enjoyed at any time on any clear day. Across the Bay, you can just barely see by eye on a clear day the Provincetown Monument and the sands of that area. A bit to the right are the shores of Wellfleet and then Eastham. To the left of the

Monument and far over the Bay, the cliffs of the shores of Plymouth can be seen. Further to the left you can see the wind turbines at the military reservation in Sandwich and at Massachusetts Maritime Academy in Buzzards Bay, as well as the Sagamore Bridge and the Canal Generating Plant located there. Closer, you can see the shores of Dennis directly ahead, and the shores of Yarmouth toward the left. Just a few hundred yards from the tower, as you look north toward the

Bay, you can see Scargo Lake itself; shaped a bit like a fish. The Lake is about 60 acres in size with a maximum depth of 48 feet. Looking south from the Tower, you are looking over South Dennis toward West Dennis; the farthest water tower is on Route 28. The next farthest is on Airline Road in South Dennis, so you are looking over the entire width of the mid-Cape area here.

The lake itself is named after the Nobscusset Princess Scargo; folklore has it that she had her father dig the lake for her pet fish that she had been given by a suitor as a gift – the hill was thus made from digging the lake out. We know now, though, that the hill area was actually formed by the Wisconsin Glacier tens of thousands of years ago. Rocks and gravel piled high along the north side of Cape Cod in this area at that time; this "moraine" runs along and north of Route 6 from Brewster to Sandwich. Looking to the south, towards South and West Dennis, you are looking over the flatter "outwash plain," lower sandy areas formed from waters rushing off the glacier toward the south.

Scargo Tower was first built in 1874 as a wooden observation tower for tourists. A 5 cent admission was charged and the telescope on the tower could see the church clock in Provincetown. As a result of the open exposure of Scargo Hill to the heavy winds, the structure was destroyed in a gale in 1876. Subsequently, the structure was rebuilt, only to be burned down in 1900. The present structure, built from boulders barged here from Sandy Neck, was opened in 1902, and has withstood the tests of time. If you look just above the entry door, there is a plaque that explains that the Hill and Tower were donated to the Town of Dennis in 1929 in memory of the Tobey family.

Directions: From Route 134, go north from the Mall area to the Police Station, turning left on Bob Crowell Road, and then right onto Bass River Road. Take Bass River Road 2.2 miles to Scargo Hill Road, a sharp right. The Tower is on the left at 152 Scargo Hill Road; just take the steep drive directly up to the Tower parking.

Google Map QR Code:

About QR Codes:

Use a QR code reader app on your phone or tablet to scan the QR code here. It will immediately take you directly to a detailed Google driving map showing the Tower's exact location. QR apps are free and easy to use and can be downloaded from Apple or GooglePlay. More information about QR codes is found on page 95.

Hokum Rock

A short distance from Scargo Hill is the Hokum Rock area, on the south side of Hokum Rock Road. There is free parking here for several cars. The rock formation is about 14.5 feet high and about 100 feet around and composed of several dozen large boulders; there are several small overhangs that make the area most interesting. While the rocks and caves are the main attraction for just viewing or careful climbing, there is also a set of hiking trails out behind the rocks.

It is the Hokum Rock legends that bring most here to wonder just what had gone on in this area in the past. While this is now a residential setting, in the past, it was a fairly remote part of the town. There are two different legends. One is that the area was named for the Nobscusset native Hoken who lived in this area; court records from 1674 indicate that he had been convicted of burglary and

theft and breaking out of prison. A second legend goes that in the 1800's, a descendant of the Nobscussets had lived as a hermit in the small caves here at Hokum Rock. When anyone came near his cave dwelling, he supposedly called out "Who comes?" and that is where the name "Hokum" came from.

The rocks themselves are called glacial erratics, large boulders left by the motions of the Cape Cod Bay lobe of the Laurentide ice sheet between 10,000 to 25,000 years ago. The rocks were probably formed about 300 million years ago, and then were moved by the glacier's conveyer-belt motion from north of Boston or even perhaps New Hampshire or Maine; you can still see markings on the rocks from the motions of the glacier, while other markings are due to erosion since then. Most references indicate that the rock is "granite," but the bronze plaque at the site, recently erected by the Dennis Historic Commission, indicates that it is diorite, which is slightly different than other granites. The plaque is not on the actual Hokum rocks, but on an added marker stone. You can find many smaller glacial erratics along the north side of the Cape and even into Eastham (Doane Rock). The famous Plymouth Rock is also a glacial erratic.

Unfortunately, the hiking trails behind and to the left of the rock are not very well marked, and easy to confuse. Many trail intersections make the area a challenge. It is best to use a GPS if you can. At the same time, there are several miles of trails here, and you can end up at beautiful views of Simmons Pond, about 0.8 miles to the southeast through the woods. As you enter the sand area, keep to the right until you are just out of the sand pit, then turn left and stay straight from there to reach serene Simmons pond. The sand pits in the area are town public works sandpits.

Directions: From Route 134, go north from the Mall area past the Police Station and then about 1.3 miles north to Hokum Rock Road on the left. Take Hokum Rock Road to Hokum Rock parking area, just past 135 Hokum Rock Road, on the left.

Google Map QR Code:

Nobscusset Conservation Area

Often called by the older name "Indian Lands," this 23-acre parcel provides beautiful overlooks of Bass River from the east shores of the River in South Dennis. There is plenty of parking at the former town-hall parking area on Main Street, South Dennis, at the bike trail. From there, it is just a short 0.3 miles walk along the new bike trail toward Yarmouth to reach the entrance to the actual conservation area on the left.

Several paths lead into two peninsulas in the conservation area. Staying to the left on the main path after entering the area brings you to a half-mile loop, the Lady Slipper Trail, in the south pen-insula; the loop takes you right along the shores of Bass River, with spectacular views to the south and east  of the opposite shores of Yarmouth. The bridge between Den-nis and Yarmouth on Highbank Road can easily be seen as well. Instead of turning left on the original path, turning right, then staying straight, will bring you into the northern peninsula; this loop (Nickerson Point Trail) brings you through fine white pine stands (white pines were the native pines when the Nobscussets lived here) and to a high embankment along the shore of Bass River and then along a marshy area and back to your starting point. Bass River itself was formed during the Wisconsin glacier, from huge meltwater runoff from the glacier. It is about 7 miles in length, extending nearly all the way across the Cape, separating Dennis and Yarmouth. It is the largest tidal river on Cape Cod, and forms an important ecosystem, supporting a large and diverse population of fish, shellfish, animals, and plants.

For centuries, this area had been used as a winter haven by the Nobscusset natives. During the summer, they would farm in the area north of Scargo Lake, between the Lake and Cape Cod Bay. There, they would grow corn, beans and squash in the good soil in that area, using crabs and fish to help nourish the crops. Because the area on the north side is so exposed to winter storms, they would then move after harvest time to the area in South Dennis, along the eastern shore of Bass River. Here they would have warm and protected structures in which they lived for the winter. When the English settlers arrived, the Nobscussets were very friendly and lived in peace. But they were forced to live the ways of the settlers, and over the years, the tribe dwindled from around 120 in 1685 to virtually nothing by 1800; by then, there were 1,400 settlers in

Dennis. A tiny Nobscusset burial ground, with no stones, but surrounded by a fence and marked with a simple plaque, exists on the north shore of Scargo Pond, directly across from Osprey Lane.

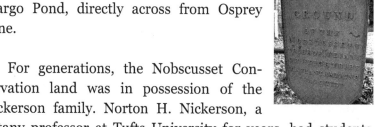

For generations, the Nobscusset Conservation land was in possession of the Nickerson family. Norton H. Nickerson, a botany professor at Tufts University for years, had students come every summer, staying in housing on his property on Bass River Road, and doing research at the river and elsewhere on Cape Cod. In the spring, he would often lead walks through the area, showing people the many different species of plants there, from the white pines to the hundreds of lady slippers. Nickerson was also Chairman of the Dennis Conser-

vation Commission, and in the 1980's offered the land to the Town. When there was little progress, he sold the land to a developer who planned condominiums on the site; Nickerson, an ardent environmentalist, knew that this would be motivation enough to the townspeople to acquire the property, which they did. The Nobscussets and Nickerson, too, revered the land and deeply respected the rights of all others to enjoy the beauty and serenity of this place; hopefully all that use this conservation area today can do those things as well.

Directions: From Route 134, go north from the Mall area and turn left on Bob Crowell Road, just before the Police Station. At the end of Crowell Road, turn left onto Bass River Road, and proceed over the bridge straight onto Main Street and then around the bend to the parking area on the right.

Google Map QR Code:

Johnny Kelley Recreation Area

C onveniently located just a short distance from Route 134 in South Dennis is the 25-acre Johnny Kelley Recreation area, a four-season location with facilities for use by all ages. Four lighted tennis courts, 2 basketball courts, soccer and baseball fields, a walking/ running track, an ex-

ercise course with modern exercise stations, a full playground, a picnic area with grills, and restrooms are available to all. Ample parking is found on either the Bob Crowell Road or Bass River Road accesses to the area.

The walking and exercise paths have full handicap access and total 1 miles in length, 0.4 for the shorter northern loop and 0.6 for the longer southern loop. They are wide, well-maintained paths through the shady pine oak woods that are common in the area; this gives the walking area a very natural, woodland feeling. Around the perimeter of the shorter loop is a Braille trail with guiding ropes and explanatory signs. All the playing fields are in excellent condition and well maintained; tennis courts were just recently built. The playground is a spacious and shady one, with a woodchip base and recently upgraded equipment – children will find many interesting activities there. Cooking grills and picnic tables are in the pavilion just past the playground area.

The area itself was named in honor of Johnny Kelley, who had represented the U.S. in the Olympics in 1936 and 1948; Runner's World Magazine named Kelley as runner of the century in 2000. A long-time resident of Dennis after his retirement from work with Boston Edison Company, Kelley competed in 61 Boston Marathons, and could often be seen training along the roadways in Dennis, running 50 miles a week. Even at age 70 he said that he was afraid to stop running, that he felt so good doing it. Kelley won the Boston Marathon two times, in 1935 and 1945, came in second place seven times, and ran his last marathon at the age of 84 years; all that he did served as motivation and pride for everyone in Dennis. A long-time advocate of good health and exercise, Kelley lived until he was 97 years of age, in 2004.

The area serves as a community recreation area and is a focus of many activities, year round. Many youth and adult teams practice sports or play here during afternoons or week-ends. During the summer, the area is used each day by local youth day camps sponsored by the Town but remains open to the public. Each fall on Veterans' Day, the AMVETS and the Dennis Chamber of Commerce set up a sea of flags that fills the athletic fields, honoring veterans as well as first responders and others. It is an especially inspiring sight to walk the track at that time. In September, the Chamber of Commerce sponsors a family Field Day at the area, with free food for all, sack races and other games, face painting — definitely a wonderful time for all.

Directions: From Route 134, go north from the Mall area and turn left on Bob Crowell Road, just before the Police Sta-

tion. Just before the end of Crowell Road, turn left into the parking area for the Kelley Recreation area. An additional parking area is just around the corner to the left.

Google Map QR Code:

T he Dennis north side beaches include Chapin Beach, Mayflower Beach, Bayview Beach, Corporation Beach, Howes Street Beach, Harbor View Beach, Cold Storage Beach, and Sea Street Beach.

During the day in the summer, it can be difficult to park at these beaches. Beach parking stickers are required for parking from the Saturday before Memorial Day through Labor Day; at other times of the year, you may park during the day in the parking areas with no fees. Beach stickers for parking in Beach lots can be obtained at the Town Hall; stickers can be purchased on weekdays, and also on Saturdays on Sunday mornings. You can also pay a daily fee at the lot instead, but it is much cheaper to get a weekly or seasonal sticker. Most beaches require stickers in the summer from 7 a.m. – 5 p.m.

A great time to visit the north side beaches is the hours from 5 p.m. – 8 p.m. The sunsets over the waters of Cape Cod Bay are nothing short of outstanding, the sun and water are still very enticing, and a great reason to visit at this time; all of the beaches offer 180-degree views of the Bay, with Eastham and Wellfeet toward the right, the shores of Plymouth directly across the Bay, and Yarmouth, Barnstable, and Sandwich to the left, along the shore.

The Dennis north side beaches do differ slightly from one another, and thus it is a great adventure to visit one each  evening during a vacation stay. All of the beaches have very large tidal changes and this results in sand flats that can be walked out on at low tide; check a tide chart via Google to find when the tide is going out so that you can enjoy this popular activity in leisure. During the off hours, there is plenty of room on the beaches for Frisbee, small soccer games or other games, kite flying, skim boarding, having a picnic supper, or just enjoying the beach walking, collecting shells, looking at the diversity of living things in the tidal pools, and enjoying the beautiful scenery. (Some of these activities are not allowed during the bathing day; check with the guard on duty if not sure.) The sand on these beaches is in general very fine, with few rocks in most locations; this makes for great beach walking. Most beaches in this area are located between areas of private property, so be sure to respect those private property lines. Animals are not allowed on the Dennis beaches or parking areas from Memorial Day through Labor Day, so it is best to walk your dog elsewhere.

With currents that bring water from the north into the Bay, water temperatures in the Bay are slightly lower than on the southside beaches. Tidal range is larger, though, resulting in a greater ability to view tidal flats and pools. During the off season, this area can be subjected to very fierce storms with heavy winds from the northeast and pounding surf as a result; the surf can easily reach the uppermost parts of the beaches. This is an increasingly difficult problem not only for homeowners along the water but also for the town in maintaining the public beaches and preventing their serious degradation. During the placid summer months it is easy to forget how harsh this environment can be in other months; we all need to be mindful of this, and do our utmost to avoid contributing to erosion of the beach. The simple beachgrass plants really do help in this regard, and they often have runners growing unseen below the sand surface, many feet from where the plants are seen above the ground. Staying far away from all vegetation, and not walking on sand slopes are key steps to take in helping to avoid this beach erosion.

Directions: Chapin, Mayflower, and Bayview beach are all accessed in Dennis village from Route 6A by taking Beach Street, directly across from the Dennis Public Market. Corporation and Howes Street beaches are accessed at the end of Corporation Road, just east of Dennis Village on Route 6A. To reach Harbor View, from East Dennis Take Bridge Street to Sesuit Neck Road. To reach Cold Storage Beach, and Sea Street Beach, from East Dennis, take School Street to either North Street or Cold Storage Road.

Google Map QR Code:

Bass River Park

The Bass River Park is located in West Dennis, just east of the Bass River Bridge on Route 28. Here you can enjoy 180-degree scenic views of Bass River where you can watch birds, people, and boating. Boardwalks provide for each access to the shore area. There are several viewing benches as well as protected picnic areas along the boardwalk. During the summer, there are also kayak rentals and paddleboard rentals to provide access for all to this important environmental resource.

The River itself is an estuary and important ecological and recreational area; it forms a boundary between much of Dennis and Yarmouth, and flows 7 miles from Follins Pond to the shoreline. The River was formed originally during the times of

the last glacier, from 10,000 to 25,000 years ago, from meltwater runoff from the glacier which stalled just to the north. The marshes along Bass River provide critical habitat and nutrients for many fish and shellfish. The Division of Marine Fisheries has identified over forty species of fish in Bass River, including, of course, bass.

Bass River bridge itself, a traditional photo and fishing spot for years, is just a short walk from the Park, but stay on the sidewalks and use caution along very busy Route 28. Just east is Merrill Veterans' Memorial Park, recently redesigned. There, many Veterans' activities and ceremonies are held each year; a beautiful boardwalk into the marsh is found there as well. Further east is the town boat ramp; together these areas provide for nearly 6 acres of waterfront property along Bass River, for all to enjoy.

From the Bass River Park area, we can look to see South Yarmouth on the western shore of the River, just past the Bass River Bridge. Directly across the water in the distance is the Blue Rocks Golf  Course in South Yarmouth. The area to the right of the park is the Cove Road and Horsefoot Cove area of West Dennis. A great area to observe the River, where you can look over to South Dennis, is 0.5 miles straight up on Cove Road (turn left from the Park, then take the first left, at an angle, after you leave the Park).

The Park area is a sustainable ecological park, where several types of natural ecosystems intersect: salt marsh, Atlantic cedars, and sand dunes. Considerable attention was made in designing the area to improve drainage by reducing the amount of asphalt paving, and using more permeable construction, as well as relying on natural drainage areas. The Park itself has been the source of some controversy. For many years, the area had been a commercial location, with many different businesses and restaurants having been there, and some residents did not want that changed. The Park property was acquired by the Town in 2005 for $3.2 million and was rezoned as a marine open space district for recreational and light water use. The landscape design and construction cost another $1 million, with design work by Stoss Landscape Urbanism. The rolling hills near the street had been frequently criticized as creating an unnatural view for the location, and were eventually lowered to improve the view. Some residents have also objected to even the light commercial activity (rentals) on the Town property.

Crossing the River to South Yarmouth was first made easier in 1795 when a ferry service to cross the river was started at this location; the craft was poled across the river for two cents for passengers and 25 cents for carriages. (Ferry Street is the road just north of Route 28 on the east side of the River.) In the early 1800's, shipbuilding and other commerce was found in this area, and the area was an important harbor, as it is today. The first bridge here was a wooden toll bridge with a drawbridge, built in 1832. A second bridge, with a large earthen dam in the middle of the river, was built in 1907. The current bridge was built in 1935 and is scheduled to be replaced in 2020. The closest crossing of the river is on Highbank Road, several miles to the north. There was also at one time a bridge at the end of Cove Road, over to South Dennis, but that was ruined by ice in the early 1900's.

Directions: Take Route 28 in West Dennis west toward South Yarmouth. About 1/2 mile past the church on the right, just before Bass River Bridge, is the Bass River Park Area. The parking area is large and readily accessible.

Google Map QR Code:

N early every elementary school has a playground, but that can be a little hit or miss in terms of what you might find. Some of the best playgrounds in the area can be found at the following locations. Check out one each day for a guaranteed thumbs up from the kids!

West Dennis – This fully accessible and popular playground is probably one of the nicest playgrounds in the area, with recycled rubber base and all modern, interesting equipment. It is located behind the West Dennis Community Building on School Street in West Dennis, with excellent parking. (Built in 1867, and recently restored fully as a National Historic Building, the building served as the West Dennis Graded Schoolhouse in the late 1800's. There is a small but interesting

historical museum here that is open a few hours a week during the summer).

West Dennis – There is a popular playground just to the right of the Baker School on Route 28, with ample parking, classic swing set for all ages, and several playing fields and ball fields. Don't miss the playground for younger children at the bottom of the hill. (The Baker School was constructed in 1931 at a cost of $81,500, with a large addition added in 1951.)

Dennis Port – The wonderful Mike Stacey Playground on Hall Street, just off Route 28, is adjacent to a large, pleasant park area. The playground itself has some unique playthings, in a new area with a wood shaving base. The area is conveniently located, just one block from Dennis Port shops and Dennis Library. There is a small parking area along the street with additional parking across the street.

South Dennis – Johnny Kelley Park has a spacious, shady playground that is great for younger children, with a full swingset and many other activities. There are also large playing fields, picnic and cooking area, tennis courts and several basketball courts. Walking and exercise paths and a path for the blind are also available. There is excellent parking, right off Bob Crowell Road, just off Route 134.

South Yarmouth – Station Avenue Elementary School has a fine playground with plenty of parking and lots of play options for the kids. Basketball hoops, a full swing set, hopscotch, and large playing fields are also found here. The play area is just to the right of the school building, just south of Route 6 on Station Avenue.

South Yarmouth – Peter Homer Park on Old Townhouse Road, just off Station Avenue, has a nice playground with excellent parking. This is a large recreation area with many playing fields and is right at start of the Cape Cod Rail Trail and Yarmouth Bike Trail. Restrooms are available near this popular play area and there is some seating for parents.

West Barnstable – Luke's Love Playground in West Barnstable is a Boundless Playground with activities for children of all abilities; it provides universal access pathways and surfaces. Modern equipment. and rubber mat surfacing with some wood chips makes for a great play area. There are two play areas, one for ages 2-5 and one for older children up to 12. Swings, climbing walls, several slides, music area, and many different activities are found at Luke's Love Playground as well as a beautiful garden area and good picnic seating for parents. There is also softball/baseball/kickball field. All together, just 0.8 miles north of Route 6 on Route 149 (exit 5) this is a great preemptive stop before heading onto Route 6!

Google Map QR Code:

Main Street, Dennis Port

The village of Dennis Port extends from Swan Pond River to the Harwich town line, south to the ocean beaches, and north to Upper County Road. Visitors can easily think of Dennis Port as just a path to somewhere else, especially when traveling on Route 28, but the area is really worthy of a visit for its own sake.

Dennis Port was for many years a thriving center for fishing in the region. In the 1840's, there were many employed in cod and mackerel fishing from several wharves off the south side of Dennis in Crocker's Neck, later called Dennis Port. It was not an easy life, though, with fishing catches declining consistently through the 1800's and with several deadly gales,

such as the one in October 1851 that killed many Dennis fishermen in their vessels off of Prince Edward Island. Now there are only small craft using the waters of Dennis Port.

On the land, Dennis Port grew in the 1800's to be the main center of business for not just Dennis, but for Harwich and Yarmouth as well. Indeed, in 1862, Ginn's Bazaar, really the first strip mall in the town, had five stores in one building, with offices upstairs. The entire area was destroyed in a fire in 1931, but was quickly replaced with some of the now still-standing buildings. There were two pharmacies, a music store, a hardware store, several restaurants, a barber shop, and even a seasonal chicken pie store. The area thrived until the 1980's, when the Patriot Square Mall was built in South Dennis. Then, the Dennis Port business area languished until just recently when it was revitalized by the many businesses in the area.

Most would want to see Dennis Port in two ways, partly by car, and partly on foot. As you cross into Dennis Port from West Dennis and come around "the bend", you will find a great miniature golf area, perfect for some afternoon or evening fun; also a wood products store that is fantastic for rainy-day browsing. Right at the same location on Holiday Hill is a popular and classic ice cream stand, owned and run by the same family for many years. Further down on Route 28 are several pizza locations and several other restaurants.

Behind the businesses here, and extending all the way to Upper Country Road and up behind Hart Farm, is an extensive area of cedar and fresh-water marsh called "The Plashes". The area drains toward the west, then directly into Swan Pond River. Years ago, children would skate in this area, but in recent years, it has been totally closed off to the public. The 2.5 mile Swan Pond River itself is a tidal river, and like Bass River, it is a glacial outwash river from thousands of years ago; it extends from Nantucket Sound all the way to Swan Pond

which is just north of Upper Country Road, behind Clancy's. The Plashes area also extends south of Route 28 to Lower County Road.

The main commercial center of Dennis Port is best enjoyed on foot, and there is excellent municipal parking behind the commercial center that provides access to the area. You can find just about anything you might want in Dennis Port, so it is a great place to visit on a summer day or evening. You can find everything from jewelry to second hand goods to candy, home furnishings, furniture, gifts, cards, a dog wash, music lessons and instruments, yoga lessons, a barber shop. There are several restaurants in the area, general and grocery stores, as well as several discount-type stores. Several art studios are found right on Main Street in Dennis Port as well, and some of the art is even found on murals that can be enjoyed by all outside the buildings.

Not to be missed is the practical but important laundromat behind and to the south of the commercial area. The Dennis Public Library is just south of the main commercial area as well, and offers a wealth of services including wifi, computer access, current newspapers and, of course, books to borrow. The Dennis Port Village Green, also south and behind the commercial area, is an inviting place for a quiet picnic or just a place to relax or play; summer concerts are held here Tuesday and Friday evenings. Dennis Port is a wonderful place to spend several hours during your stay, an inviting spot with real Cape Cod flavor and history. Don't miss it!

Directions: Take Route 28 in West Dennis west toward Harwich. Just past the Dennis Fire Station and the water tower on the left, just after the lights, you will cross Swan Pond River. Dennis Port extends along Route 28 from here to Harwich, south to the ocean, and north to Upper County Road.

Google Map QR Code:

Bass Hole Boardwalk

B ass Hole Boardwalk in Yarmouth Port offers some of the finest sunset views anywhere in the Mid-Cape region. The 868-foot long boardwalk extends directly across hundreds of acres of salt marsh at Chase Garden Creek and affords incredible views of Chapin Beach in Dennis to the right and Sandy Neck Beach to the left. Both Chapin and Sandy Neck are important barrier beaches protecting the critical salt marsh and upland ecosystems behind them. The buildings that you can see on Chapin are the Aquaculture Research Corporation, a shellfish hatchery that grows oysters and clams. These are subsequently released to shellfish beds all around the region, to continue growth there, until they are eventually harvested.

On Sandy Neck itself, there is a remote "colony" of several dozen homes just behind and to the left of the lighthouse that you can see from the Boardwalk; these homes are only accessible via water or via a 6-mile over-sand route. The lighthouse, 40 feet high, was built in 1857. The large structure to the left of the boardwalk is an osprey nesting area. The marsh itself is a critical ecosystem and environment, providing nutrients and food for many fish and animals that depend on the area; it is a favorite activity of all to watch from the boardwalk for fish and crabs in the marsh just a few feet below. At the end of the boardwalk is an observation area where you can sit and enjoy the gorgeous views and breezes.

On the small hill just behind the parking area is a picnic and cooking pavilion, a great place for a picnic. There is also a small playground that the children will love. To the front right of the parking area is access to a handicap-accessible area that provides winding boardwalks with closeup views of the marsh and cedar swamp areas. An extensive trail system (Callery-Darling trails) is also in this area. One trail is accessible just past the playground area, at the right corner of the open area. A few hundred yards up this trail you will find another shorter boardwalk over Chase Garden Creek, and an even quieter place to enjoy the marsh scenery; this trail loops around through pitch pine woods and then through a fine cedar swamp, well worth seeing.

There are several miles of trails in the Callery-Darling system, and there is a map of the trails near the parking area. Taking the trail on the opposite side of the road from the parking area, then turning right will bring you through highlands along the marsh with wonderful views along the way. The combination of fresh water marshes and salt water marshes here allows for a large diversity of plants and animals, making the ecosystems here most interesting to see.

The small crescent-shaped beach here, Gray's Beach, is a favorite of local families, and while small, the beach adds yet another attraction that makes this entire area a spot not to be missed. At low tide, the water is so far out that the beach is mostly sand and small pools that are great for small children.

The area here, north of the hilly moraine material left by the glacier thousands of years ago, was formed by deposits from the large lake between the glacier and the moraine itself.

With the shallow waters and marsh seen here now, it is hard to believe that this area was at one time a full harbor. During the early- to mid-1700's, there was even shipbuilding here by the Bray Family, with fishing schooners as large as 100 tons being built here. Silting in of the harbor, though, due to storms and the moving sands, reduced its usefulness for large ships, and the small boating presence here now is only a small reminder of what once was. A fascinating legend about this area is that Leif Ericson's brother, Thorvald, had visited this area in the year 1003. He was shot by an arrow in a dispute with the natives, and as he lay dying, he had named the area "Crossness," and requested that he be buried on one of the hillsides here. Unfortunately, it is not known if this really did happen, or if it did, exactly where. Still, it provides for some interesting reflection on the past as we look back from the Boardwalk to the pine-covered hillsides here.

Directions: Take Center Street from Route 6A. Continue to the end of Center Street; the parking for the beach, the boardwalk, the picnic, playground area, and the trials is all found at the end of the street on the right.

Google Map QR Code:

Yarmouth Botanic Trails

A hidden gem in Yarmouth Port, just behind the U.S. Post Office, are the 50 acres of Botanic Trails owned by the Yarmouth Historic Society. The entrance to the area is a tiny driveway just to the right of the Post Office area. There is parking for just a small number of vehicles. Right near the parking area are several interesting things to see. The beech tree there is nearly 200 years old, and provides a fantastic place for a quiet family picnic and time to reflect on what once was. The Tufts gatehouse itself houses an 18th-century loom  that is displayed during the summer months. The small circular herb garden is a delight to see in all seasons, and is maintained by the Garden Club of Yarmouth. The Yarmouth Historic Society can provide historic information about Yarmouth and maintains an archive, library, and information center in the Gorham Cobbler Shop building that you pass on the entrance driveway; in the 1800's, this building was located just next to the Parnassus Bookstore, just to the left on Route 6A. Just up the hill to the left of the Gate House is the Captain Bangs Hallet House, open to the public.

The Botanic Trail property and the Hallet house were given to the Historic Society in 1953 by Guido Perera, a direct descendent of Anthony Thacher who had been one of the first settlers in the Yarmouth area, in 1639. During the 1890's, there was actually a private golf course that the Thacher descendants had used on this property. As you travel through the woods, you will not see any open greens, for sure, but you can see several flattened hilltops, and can, with some imagination, imagine what once was here, now long overgrown with trees.

The trail itself starts to the left of the gatehouse as a level gravel drive. A few yards into the walk, the trail forks. Both trails lead to Miller's Pond, about 0.7 miles distant. The trail to the left ascends a small hill through an area with many wildflowers; the goldenrod here is particularly noteworthy in the fall, but there are flowers during each season. To the left on the hillside are some fine sugar maples as well as beech trees. A little further along the path is a large stand of rhododendrons, a sight not to be missed when they are in bloom in the spring. As you travel on the path, you will see many different plant species including pitch pine, white pine, white oak, red oak, a few spruce trees, blueberries, hollies and many wild plants including Lady's slippers. The path winds through the woodlands, and is generally fairly level. Eventually a staircase is reached that will take you down close to the shore of Miller Pond. The main path runs right along the side of the pond, and then trends upward a bit to reach the right fork of the original trail near the Chapel.

Taking the trail to the right instead of to the left at the original fork will bring you in just a few yards to the Kelley Chapel. This charming building in a very open area is a worthy goal in itself. Built in 1873 by David Kelley for his mourning daughter and as a non-sectarian place of worship, the building was moved here in 1960 from the original location in South Yarmouth next to the Quaker Meeting House there. Inside are very spartan fixtures including the pews, a woodstove, and an organ. From this area, the trail ascends slightly and then winds through the woods to reach the shore of Miller Pond.

Miller Pond itself was formed as a glacial kettle pond, when a large chunk of ice from the glacier, embedded in the surface debris, was left to melt. The pond itself has many frogs and turtles and other wildlife nearby, but apparently no fish have lived in the pond for some time.

There are no buildings here at all, just peace and serenity Although the occasionally noisy railway is just a few hundred yards away, this can actually help to bring us back in time – the railroad in this area had been in existence since the 1850's. The pond drains on the opposite shore through some small dikes. The pond was named for John Miller who had served, with some criticism by townspeople for his outspoken ways, as the second minister in the town, beginning the mid 1640's.

A second trail loop, about equal in length to the first, runs from either side of the pond, around and behind the pond, and makes a great addition to your walk. Be careful at the eastern part of the pond; there are several trails there that leave the Botanic Trails area, and finding the right trail to head back to the Gatehouse can be a little confusing in that area. Be sure to go up the stairs to be heading in the right direction from that location.

Directions: On Route 6A in Yarmouth Port, locate the U.S. Post Office in Yarmouth Port. Take the small, easy-to-miss driveway immediately to the right of the Post Office. Continue past the Yarmouth Historic Society building on the right to the Gatehouse right near the large beech tree. Park in this area, using caution to avoid blocking the narrow roadway.

Google Map QR Code:

Captains' Mile and More

During the 1800's, more than 50 sea captains built their stately homes in a short stretch of about 1 mile along what is now Route 6A in Yarmouth Port; other sea captains lived in the Bass River area of South Yarmouth, and in many other Cape towns as well. A walk along Route 6A in this area is a way to travel back in time. The period from 1800 to 1870 was one of strong commercial maritime activity, with commercial schooners from Cape Cod traveling to Asia, to South America and Africa, and to Europe as well. Packet boats sailed to New York and Boston. The resulting wealth is reflected in the stately homes built here during those times. There are also some more modest homes from earlier periods, Capes and half-Capes, as the area had been settled by the English settlers as early as 1639. Parking at the Botanic Trails parking is best, as traffic is fast in this area, and parking locations are few.

The Captain Bangs Hallet House is just a short walk up the hill that is a continuation of the driveway into the Botanic Trails parking area (no driving, though). The Hallet house is a fine Greek Revival home built in 1840 by the Thacher family that had settled in this area in the 1600's. A smaller home had existed here previously, build in 1740, but Hallet expanded that considerably in 1840. In front of the home is the beautiful Yarmouth Port village green and Strawberry Lane. The home was later lived in by Captain Allen Hinkley Knowles and then later by Captain Bangs and Anna Hallet during their retirement starting in 1863. During the summer, the home is open for tours by the Historic Society several hours each day.

The best way to see all the sea captains' homes is to take the walking tour along Route 6A, which provides a step by step guide to 53 different sea captain's homes in just a short mile walk. While the traffic is heavy along Route 6A these days, the sidewalk walk is the only way to truly appreciate what was here so many years ago. It is best to walk on the north sidewalk. You can see a few glimpses of the ocean as you walk, and it is easy to imagine the far away places that brought wealth to this area so long ago. Early morning in this area is a real delight, with much less traffic. Each captain's home is marked with  a plaque with schooner on it. While the homes are private residences and not open to the public, they can be admired and photographed from the sidewalk area.

A detailed, house-by-house guide is provided by the Yarmouth Historic Society; you can access it using the special QR code at the end of this section and view it as you walk. One example is the stately home of Captain Asa Eldredge, found at 100 Route 6A. Eldredge sailed the majestic clipper ship, the *Red Jacket*, to all corners of the world, and had even won a speed competition in 1854 in travelling from New York to Liverpool. In 1856, when just 47 years old, he died at sea aboard the steamship Pacific, enroute from Liverpool to New York, most likely having hit an iceberg in the north Atlantic. A picture of Eldredge is found in the Bangs Hallet house.

In addition to the sea captains' homes, there are several other interesting homes in this area. Anthony Thacher had  settled here first in 1639 with his new family when his children had all been in a shipwreck just off Rockport when they first arrived in America in 1635. His son John, was born in 1638 in Marblehead and married in 1664. The John Thacher home, built by Anthony for John at that time, is still present at the corner of Thacher Street and Route 6A, across from the Post Office. The home was originally built a short distance away on Thacher Street and was then moved here in 1680. John was active in town government and in the militia for many years. The original structure is just the very eastern section of the home, near the back; much of what is seen from the street was added at a later time.

The Winslow Crocker House is a fine example of eighteenth century Georgian colonial architecture; Crocker was a wealthy investor, and as a result the house is much larger and more elaborate than the typical homes of the time. The home

was originally built in 1780 six miles away in West Barnstable, but was moved to Yarmouth in 1936 by Mary Thacher who lived on Boston's Beacon Hill; she renovated the home extensively, so it is not exactly as it was in 1780, and she used it to house her eclectic collection of colonial rugs, furniture, ceramics, pewter, and other antiques. The house is open during the summers a few hours each week for visitors.

As you walk in this area, be sure to stop at Hallet's. Hallet's first opened in 1889, as a full pharmacy and soda fountain. Most of the original equipment is still in place, and you can thus travel back in time and order a soda, a sandwich, and ice cream. Also, be sure to see the Parnassus Book store, which has been operated by the Muse family for decades.

Directions: On Route 6A in Yarmouth Port, locate the U.S. Post Office in Yarmouth Port. Take the small, easy-to-miss driveway immediately to the right of the Post Office. Continue past the Yarmouth Historic Society building on the right to the Gatehouse right near the large beech tree. Park in this area, using caution to avoid blocking the narrow roadway.

Google Map QR Code:

Captains' Mile Walking Tour Map:
*This saves a PDF file to your phone
or tablet, then you need to open the PDF.*

Peter G. Homer Recreation Area

T he Peter G. Homer Park, previously known as the Old Town House Park, is found, with excellent parking, just a short distance up Old Town House Road, in South Yarmouth. Here you can find wonderful facilities and activities that can make for a great and healthful time for all. The area is adjacent to the Bayberry Hills Golf course, found at the end of Old Town House Road. In 1835, town members had set up a town house in this area, for government functions of the town, hence the name of the road itself. In 1873, a large fire had burned in this area, destroying nearly a mile square of forest land.

The Park itself now is accessible year round and offers many recreation options. The fields to the right of the parking area include two softball/baseball fields and two soccer fields.

The athletic fields are well maintained, and a busy place for soccer and little league, and other youth sports in season. Visitors are welcome to use the fields for casual recreation year round. The park is also the start of the Cape Cod Rail Trail. A great playground

with plenty of seating for parents is found just a short distance from the parking lot, with good views of the fields as well – a perfect place for both young and older children to play.

A walking/ jogging track goes from the right of the parking area all around the athletic fields area, bringing you back to the parking area near the facilities building. The track is about 0.5 miles total length and is an easy, level, accessible walkway. To the right of the athletic fields is an industrial area. At the rear of the park, the new Cape Cod Rail Trail extends to the east past Station Avenue and then on to South Dennis. Just north of the trail is the Town Municipal Transfer station area and septic waste facility. To the left of the athletic fields area is the northernmost section of the Bayberry Hills Golf Course.

Leaving from the left of the parking area, just behind the facilities building, the Yarmouth Bike Path takes us (to the left) just over 2 miles through gently rolling terrain to Higgins

Crowell Road in West Yarmouth, where the trail currently ends. The trail first parallels Old Town House Road, with views of the golf course to the right. After crossing Forest Road (use caution here due to the heavy traffic) and the entranceway to the golf course, the trail heads south along the golf course boundary, through the pleasant pitch pine woods, and then heads west to reach Higgins Crowell Road. Also leaving from the left of the parking area, the Cape Cod Rail Trail (to the right) brings you over the Station Avenue Bridge and then through Yarmouth woodlands towards Dennis. There is a pedestrian bridge over picture-perfect Bass River that allows you to continue on the Rail Trail all the way to Wellfleet.

To the left of the parking area, there are two bocce courts, a horseshoe area, and two full basketball courts. The facilities building has restrooms as well as a food concession in season.

Directions: From Exit 8 on Route 6, go south on Station Avenue to the second set of traffic lights. Turn right here, onto Old Town House Road. The Park area is about 0.3 mile on the right.

Google Map QR Code:

Flax Pond Recreation Area

T he Flax Pond Recreation area is one that is easy to miss due to its off-the-beaten-path location, but it is well worth finding. It is located on 16.8 acres of conservation land just off White's Path in Yarmouth. There is excellent parking with handicap access here 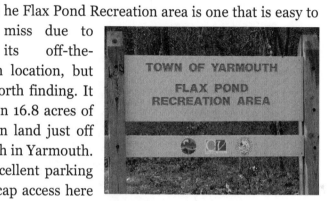 and the fresh-water swimming beach in season.

Twenty-acre Flax Pond is one of two ponds in Yarmouth that are larger than 10 acres in size. The pond has a maximum depth of about 20 feet, and has a shoreline of about 0.5 miles in length. Extensive areas of woodland surround the Pond, providing an important area for wildlife in this highly de-veloped area. The mid-Cape south of Route 6 is in general quite level, having formed as an "outwash plain" just to the south of the stalled glacier some 15,000 years ago; the melt-water during the summers would carry large amounts of sand and small stones and deposit that material as it traveled south, building the outwash plain. Ponds like Flax Pond were formed by chunks of ice left when the glacier had previously extended a bit further south. As sand-laden meltwater rushed around such blocks, small hills were formed, and we can still see these clearly in this Park area. A short trail just past the low rope area (to the left of the picnic area) leads in just a hundred yards or so into some extensive Atlantic white cedar swamp areas that are fascinating to see.

A large recreation building, Lorusso Lodge, was recently constructed at Flax Pond. Here there are meeting rooms as well as full restroom facilities. The area can seat 150 people and can be rented for meetings or gatherings year round.

To the right of the building are found four tennis courts and a basketball court. There is also a modern playground area for children near the lodge itself, and a smaller play area just past the tennis courts. A great playing field is also found on the grounds, including a ball field.

In the wooded grove behind the recreation building is found an open, pleasant picnic area with several grills and many picnic tables available; woodchips and new walkways provide a pleasant, clean surface in the area. Two large rectangular pavilion areas as well as a 37-foot gazebo also provide a great shelter for larger gatherings or outdoor meetings. The area is open to use by all if it has not been previously rented for group use; in that case, the group has use of the entire picnic area. Permission is required for groups of 15 or more.

During the summer months, an eight-week recreation program is run by the Town of Yarmouth Parks and Recreation Department for residents and non-residents aged 6 to 14. The program includes arts and crafts, archery, kayaking and canoeing, nature and science studies, team and group games, learning about traditional sports activities, special events days and many other activities. The area was once the location of Camp Kirkland, which is now located on White Rock Road on Elisha's Pond.

Paved walks from the parking area to the hill above the beach area provide easy access to the beach area. Vegetation along the shore of the pond, though, does make a walk around the pond  difficult. However, the roadway in from White's Path, which crosses the Cape Cod Rail Trail, is an easy place to walk.

Those interested in fresh water fishing can find good fishing along the shore here, for brown trout, smallmouth bass, brook trout and rainbow trout. On the far shore of the pond can be seen the Thirwood Place senior living community buildings.

Directions: From Exit 8 on Route 6, go south on Station Avenue to the first set of traffic lights. Turn left here, on White's Path. After about 0.3 miles, turn right onto Dupont Avenue, just before the cell tower. Proceed to the end of Dupont Avenue to the parking area for the Flax Pond area.

Google Map QR Code:

Judah Baker Windmill

T he Judah Baker windmill, located right on Bass River in South Yarmouth, is a wonderful place not only to view the sights of Bass River but to think about the importance that wind power has always had on Cape Cod and to reflect some on Cape Cod's past, as well.

The windmill itself was built first in Dennis in 1791 by Judah Baker (1733 – 1814), a direct Mayflower descendant. There were several mills in the area that were used to grind grain for making flour; this was the second mill in the south side of Dennis, and the only mill built in Dennis that is still standing. Originally built on the east shore of Grand Cove in South Dennis, the structure was moved several times, first to

Ferry Street in West Dennis in 1810 and then to South Yarmouth just before the Civil War, in 1863, where it was used to grind corn. At different times, the mill was on Main Street, then on River Street, in South Yarmouth. Mills were complex to build, so were often moved. Eventually, commercial flour took the place of locally ground flour, and this mill, like many others, ceased its work. Electricity took the place of wind; now we look to the wind to provide electricity. The Town of Yarmouth now owns the structure and the Historical Society of Old Yarmouth allows visitors to see the interior during the

summer months. Hours are limited, though, so it is best to call the Town of Yarmouth Visitor Center at 508-778-1008 to confirm specific hours. The entire structure has been authentically reconstructed and restored to its original condition, much as it was 225 years ago.

The mill itself now is located right on Bass River, at the end of River Street, and thus is about two miles from where it had originally been built. At the small Windmill Park, there is a parking area for several cars, grounds with wooden walkways, a sitting bench, access to the mill itself, and stairs down to a small beach along the water, best suited for tide pool investigating at low tide.

A careful look at the construction of the windmill shows that it has two dormers. One dormer is for the power shaft itself that attaches to the sail blades of the windmill. The other dormer is for a tail piece that extends to a wheel on the ground. The entire roof is supported on a set of rollers, so that the sail blades can be oriented toward the wind manually by moving the tailpiece around in a circular path around the mill. Now, the mill is fixed in place. The mill is called a "smock" windmill, since it has 8 sides, and is unusual, also, in that it has a conical cap as well. Most likely, the structure was designed by Henry Hall for Judah Baker.

Inside the mill, you can see the large wooden hopper, shoe, and damsel that direct and shake the grain into the large opening (eye) between the two granite millstones. The power of the wind is used to turn large gears with wooden teeth, that can be seen inside as well. These wooden gears mesh together and turn the shaft that connects to the moving millstone (runner stone). There is also a large wooden hook and crane system that was used to lift the upper millstone in order for it to be repaired so that it ground the grain properly. There are also numerous photos and drawings inside the building to see, and a small number of T shirts and other gift items for purchase as a remembrance of your visit to the Windmill.

The Baker windmill, besides being used for grinding grain, was used as a signal system between the north and south sides of Dennis. When the packet ship from Boston arrived at the harbor on the Dennis north side, a signal flag there could be seen from atop the windmill. In the same way, a flag was raised at the Baker windmill when an important ship arrived at Bass River, and that could be seen by those on the north side. Baker's gravesite is marked by a slate stone in the cemetery on Old Bass River Road, where the Town Hall had been for many years.

Directions: Take Route 6 to Exit 8 and turn south on Union Street/Station Avenue. Continue a total of 2.1 miles, past the high school on the left and past Long Pond on the right to the "Four Corners" intersection (near the Mercantile). At "Four Corners" intersection, continue straight across at the light. Continue 0.9 miles past the lights, turning left on River Street just after the fire station. The mill is 0.5 miles down River Street, on the left.

Google Map QR Code:

Veterans' Park, Yarmouth and Wilbur Park

J ust before the Bass River Bridge on the right is a small, pleasant park that provides a great place to watch boating activities: the Veterans' Memorial and Packet Landing Park area. There are two parking areas here, the first one for the park itself, and the second to the Town Landing area. You can park in either location and easily walk to the other.

The Veterans' Park is a pleasant place to view the Bass River and the Bass River Bridge from a unique viewpoint As close as it is to the traffic above, it is still a fine and relaxing rest spot. Several benches and a pavilion with a beautiful view make the area a great place to visit. Well-groomed landscaping, a flagpole and brick walkways make the recently redesigned area an attractive one. The Park is the location of several town ceremonies each year and is always available as a place to remember the service of our veterans or just to enjoy the scenery.

At the Town Landing area, the Town Harbormaster has a patrol boat at a year round slip, and other slips are available

and used by residents. A picnic table here is a great place for a relaxing meal with a view. This is a busy area with lots to see at any time, as Bass River has for hundreds of years been a key harbor on the south side of Dennis. In 1795, a ferry service first

brought passengers across the River from here at this landing area to the opposite shore, appropriately named – Ferry Street. The first bridge over the river was built in 1832. The current bridge was built in 1935 and is due for replacement within a few years; despite recent repairs to the bridge, you can see from this viewpoint that the bridge continues to need maintenance work each year.

Most would not know it, but the short stretch of Route 28 from the Four Corners intersection to the bridge had in the past been known, quite logically, as Bridge Street. The small lighthouse across Route 28 is not a "real" lighthouse, but was built in 1960 with a motel there at the time; it is now owned by a condominium association at that location. From the 1960's, there was a small statue of a ship's  captain standing on the side of the lighthouse just under the deck area, welcoming visitors into Yarmouth; in 2010, the "Jolly Captain," as he was known, lost his head in the wind, and was later removed entirely.

A few miles up the river from here is another park with incredible views, the Wilbur Park area. This is accessible on the Yarmouth side of the Highbank Bridge. Here there is easy parking and several benches to watch the boating activity and see the beautiful scenery. Like the Veterans' park, Wilbur Park affords an opportunity to get away from the traffic and see things from a unique perspective. With its high location along the water, it is a great spot for a picnic – cool breezes and stunning views! The currents here are quite swift and make for challenging boating. While there is a very tiny beach area (which is not even visible at high tide!), swimming is not a great idea here due to the very swift currents coming around the bend. But the fishing pier is a great location to get closer to the water, watch the boating activity, enjoy the scenery and breezes, and even to do some fishing! Wilbur Park was recently redesigned by the Massachusetts Department of Fishery and Game and the Town of Yarmouth, and is certainly worth a visit.

Directions to Veterans' Park: Take Route 28 in South Yarmouth east toward Dennis. Just before the Bass River Bridge, turn right on Pleasant Street. The parking for Veterans' Park is immediately on the left. 100 feet further is the driveway down to additional parking for Packet Landing. Pleasant Street is one way, when leaving the parking areas, turn left, then take two rights to get back to the Four Corners intersection (street lights on Route 28).

Directions to Wilbur Park: From the Four Corners intersection (Route 28 and North Main Street in South Yarmouth), take North Main Street straight, bearing right just past the market area, then past the Quaker Meeting House and

Cemetery on the right. About 300 feet past the Meeting House, bear to the right onto Highbank Road. Follow this 1.7 miles to Wilbur Park on the right, just before the river.

Google Map QR Code for Veterans' Park:

Google Map QR Code for Wilbur Park:

Main Street, Hyannis

A great way to spend the evening or afternoon is strolling along Main Street in Hyannis. Ample parking provides for easy access to this area, and a blend of restaurant, entertainment, shopping, and tourist attractions makes for a relaxing and pleasant visit.

The area extends all the way from the Transportation Terminal at the east end to the rotary near the Melody Tent at the west end. There are nearly 150 shops and businesses in a short walking distance here: art galleries, ice cream shops, book stores, silver jewelry, clothing stores, T shirt stores, gift stores, newspaper stores, glassworks, a drum shop, honey and jelly shoppes, candy, fudge, tattoo shoppes, pizza, bistros, outdoor cafes, raw food, seafood, crepes, wings .... there is not much that you can not find here. What makes the area a popular attraction for all is the relaxed Cape Cod atmosphere and the easy pedestrian access along the entire length of the street.

At the east end of Main Street, you can find the Barnstable Town Hall and Village Green. The Town Hall building was at one time the Hyannis State Teacher's College (1897 – 1944), and was later used by Massachusetts Maritime Academy until it moved to Buzzards Bay, and until 1970 by Cape Cod Community College, which located at that time to its new campus on Route 132. From 1970 to 1976, the building was used as a middle school until it became the Town Hall in 1979. The earlier Town Hall is on Main Street near the library, and is now serving as the Kennedy Museum. The name Hyannis itself comes from the native American sachem Iyannough. He had been a friend of the new settlers in the early 1600's, but later fled from them in fear and apparently died at only 23 years of age from winter exposure. A statue of Iyannough can be found on the Village Green just behind the town hall. Iyannough

Road is Route 28 (from the Yarmouth town line to the Airport Rotary) and Route 132 all the way to Route 6A.

Strolling west past the library and Kennedy museum, there are many shops to visit along the way; the far west end of Main Street has more of the smaller, eclectic shops, but the entire street is a pleasant stroll along a well-landscaped area, with many flower plantings; despite the traffic on Main Street

itself, the area is very pedestrian-friendly with wide walkways. Many special events are held here as well, including Fourth of July activities, jazz music, steel drum bands, Pops concerts, and arts and crafts festivals on the Village Green. Just south of Main Street at 46 Pearl Street is the Guyer Barn art studios, an open showcase of local artists' work.

Main Street has been a key business area in Barnstable since the 1700's. Before the automobile, horses and carriages were common here and elm trees graced the walkways. Liggett's Drugstore, Woolworth's, W.T Grants, Bradford's Hardware (still in business), Hyannis Theater and many, many more had thrived here in the past. In 1904, more than 15 buildings were destroyed by a huge fire called the "Hyannis Conflagration," along the north side of Main Street, near Center Street. When the Cape Cod Mall opened in 1970, this brought hard times to Main Street, but recent and significant improvements to the area have created an exciting and attractive area and have made this an important place to visit. Still, for Cape Cod, Hyannis is an "urban" area, and visitors should keep an open-eye at all times.

There are several parking areas for Main Street; parallel parking, for those so inclined and lucky to get a spot, is found right along the street. There are large parking areas on North Street, just north of Main Street one block, an easy walk. Parking is also found near the Town Hall, with the entry between the Library and the Post Office. Overnight parking is not permitted in these areas.

Directions: From Exit 7 on Route 6, go south on Willow Street. At the lights on Route 28, go straight across Route 28 about 0.2 miles further to Main Street, turning right to enter the Main Street area. From Route 28 in West Yarmouth, bear to the left onto Main Street, about 0.2 miles after the Mill Pond area in West Yarmouth.

Google Map QR Code:

Kennedy Legacy Trail and Museum

In 1928, Joseph Kennedy, President John Kennedy's father, had purchased a home on the water in Hyannisport. In subsequent years, John and his brother Robert purchased several other homes in the area, creating the Kennedy "compound." It was there that Kennedy learned that he had been elected as the 35th President. Kennedy said that Cape Cod was the only place that he could find a quiet time to think, so it was common for the Kennedys to be on the Cape for summer and holiday breaks. Cape Cod really was the Kennedy home, then, even the church that the Kennedys attended is only a block from Main Street in Hyannis.

In 2012, the Town of Barnstable, along with several private and government organizations, set up the Kennedy Legacy Trail to honor the long-time friendship the Town had with the Kennedy family. The trail starts at the Kennedy Museum itself, at 397 Main Street, Hyannis and proceeds one block west on Main Street, then down Pearl Street to South Street, along South Street all the way to Aseltine Park and then to the Harbor and the Kennedy Memorial. Excellent parking is available behind the Library in the municipal parking lot.

Visitors may wish to visit the Museum itself as well, although there is an admission fee for the Museum, and some do complain that it is too high. Many photographs of the Kennedy family are displayed in the museum creating a timeline of Kennedy's life, along with other photos, videos, a family tree display, and special exhibits about the Kennedy compound, the Kennedy presidency, summers on Cape Cod, and so on. The Museum also hosts many speaking engagements and educational activities for local students; a gift shop is in the Museum as well.

Outside the front of the Museum is a statue of President Kennedy, "What Could Have Been," showing Kennedy walking barefoot along the beach near his Hyannis home. Cape Cod was where Kennedy came to be energized, to relax, and to be himself. He was instrumental in the formation of the Cape Cod National Seashore in 1961 as a way to preserve the natural beauty that he appreciated so much. The Legacy Trail itself begins right here at the statue. The Trail is a 10-station self-guided tour that highlights the key activities of the Kennedy Presidency. At each of the stations, an illustrated explanatory plaque focuses on one key area. Each plaque also includes QR codes that will automatically open audio-video explanations on your phone. The full trail is 1.6 miles long, although visiting the first 7 stations is only about half as long; the last few stations can be visited directly with closer parking available at the Harbor and the Kennedy Memorial.

Key stops on the tour are the Kennedy Museum, Main Street, Rose Gardens on Pearl Street, Francis Xavier Church on South Street, the former National Guard Armory on South Street where Kennedy had accepted the Presidential nomination, recognition stops for Kennedy's involvement in forming the Cape Cod National Seashore and the Peace Corps, the Maritime Museum, Hyannis Harbor, and the Kennedy Memorial. This is a wonderful and thought-provoking walk that brings you to several spots that are not easily accessible by car. The trail takes about an hour and a half to complete.

The Kennedy compound itself is best seen from the water; tours leave the Harbor area periodically through the day and will take you to fine views of the homes. Visitors can drive down Irving Avenue in Hyannisport but it is a disappointing trip for most, as you can only barely see just one of the buildings behind the huge hedges there. Interestingly, during the Presidency itself, Kennedy stayed at a different location on nearby Squaw Island, which the Secret Service considered to be a more secure location.

Directions: From Exit 7 on Route 6, go south on Willow Street. At the lights on Route 28, go straight across Route 28 about 0.2 miles further to Main Street, turning right to enter the Main Street area. From Route 28 in West Yarmouth, bear to the left onto Main Street, about 0.2 miles after the Mill Pond area in West Yarmouth. Parking for the Trail is just behind the Library, on the left, immediately after the Post Office.

Google Map QR Code:

Hyannis Harbor

Hyannis Harbor is a bustling area at any time of the day and all year round. The harbor itself is one of the deepest natural harbors in the area, nearly 15 feet deep, and well protected from the rougher seas by its natural location, by the islands to the south, and also by the breakwater near Kalmus Beach.

Fishing boats and scallop and lobster boats leave here early in the day and come back with their catches daily, charter boats and tour boats leave from here, and the Steamship Authority as well as a private line both provide ferry service to Martha's Vineyard and to Nantucket. Sail boats and yachts make harbor here as well. Children might even find a pirate ship docked here! There is much to see here and lots of Cape

Cod atmosphere for young and old. There is a walkway the length of the harbor that allows you to get up close to all the boats, and many benches for resting along the way.

Several restaurants are found along the harbor, most with outstanding views of the harbor itself. Cape Cod is renowned for its seafood, with striped bass, bluefish, mackerel, flounder and tuna all found in the waters just offshore. Oysters, scallops and sea clams are in abundance here, and lobsters as well. If you have a taste for seafood, there is not much better place than here at the Hyannis Harbor restaurants.

The area was originally inhabited by the Iyannough native Americans, then was settled by English settlers beginning in 1639. Early settlers focused on farming, but the natural harbor here created a perfect opportunity for fishing and seagoing. The first shipping to Boston from Hyannis began in 1690. By the early 1800's several hundred shipmasters had built homes in the Hyannis area, and the harbor was a key and busy maritime area. Warehouses and storehouses were found along the water's edge to store goods brought from overseas. Schooners travelled routinely to Europe, Africa, and Asia. Salt works, using the wind to pump the ocean water and the sun to dry it to produce salt, were found along the shores of the harbor as well. Ship building thrived here in the early 1800's, too, right where the current harbor docks are today. In 1826, at a huge cost at the time of over $800,000, a breakwater was built to protect the thriving harbor industry.

As you stroll along the harbor boardwalk itself and enjoy the vivid blue hydrangea-lined walkways, you can also visit the Hyannis Arts District Artists' Shanties. Here, local artists and craftspeople showcase their art work daily  during the summer months, from photography to paintings and drawings to handmade jewelry, to tapestry, wood carving, ceramics, knot work and more. Browsing is fascinating and free, but many of the pieces are available for sale as well. New artists are featured each week, so check back frequently! Just to the north of the harbor itself is Aseltine Park, a great place to rest and enjoy the many concerts and other activities that happen there each week.

Directions: From Exit 7 on Route 6, go south on Willow Street. At the lights on Route 28, go straight across Route 28 about 0.2 miles further to Main Street, turning right to enter the Main Street area. From Route 28 in West Yarmouth, bear to the left onto Main Street, about 0.2 miles after the Mill Pond area in West Yarmouth. Parking for the Harbor is just behind the Library, on the left, immediately after the Post Office. You can also go through that lot, turn left on South Street, then right on Ocean Street to find additional, more difficult to get in season, parking places. Library parking is free; there is a fee for parking near the Harbor.

Google Map QR Code:

Kennedy Memorial and Veterans' Park

With stunning views of Hyannis Harbor, easy parking, and beautiful and meticulously maintained grounds, the Kennedy Memorial is definitely a stop worth taking and a way to remember what once was. You can find the Kennedy Memorial about a half mile down Ocean Avenue, past the Harbor, on the same side as the Harbor itself.

John Kennedy was born in 1917 in Brookline, Mass. to a well-to-do family; he attended private schools in both Massachusetts and Connecticut. His family lived in Boston, then New York City, but had begun to spend summers in Hyannis when John was a boy. In the late 1930's, he attended Harvard and traveled extensively in Europe during the summers. During World War II, Kennedy served in the Navy in the Pacific theater and also in Panama, earned a degree of lieutenant, and commanded several patrol torpedo (PT) boats. From 1947 to 1960, Kennedy served to represent Massachusetts, first as a Congressman, and then as a Senator. In the election for the

Presidency in 1960, Kennedy faced opposition due to his Catholic religion, and stated at one point that no one had asked his religion when he had served in the Pacific. Kennedy had a natural television presence and easily won a key televised debate with Richard Nixon. The country was deeply divided on many issues, though,

including civil rights issues, and Kennedy narrowly won the popular vote and became the 35th President. The Kennedy's brought a family to the White House, with John Junior and Caroline; Jacqueline and the President created an air of royalty that the country seemed to yearn for – the years became known as "Camelot."

With youth, optimism, good looks, and political connections, Kennedy had a hopeful, forward-thinking agenda. He challenged the nation in his inauguration to follow him – "Ask not what you country can do for you, ask what you can do for your country." He presided over a time when nuclear missiles threatened the U.S. from outside and racial tension threatened it from within; he dealt with the beginnings of the Vietnam War, the division of Germany by the Berlin Wall, threats from the Soviets to bury us, threats from Fidel Castro just miles away in Cuba, and a difficult economy. While occupied with international crises, Kennedy still did preside over a lowering of taxes and a strengthening economy; he supported the civil rights movement, although had kept his distance from it at first. He began the Peace Corps, the space program that brought us to the Moon, improvements in science education in the 1960's, and locally was instrumental in the creation of the Cape Cod National Seashore.

Just months before his death, Kennedy had reflected on the world situations by saying that "world peace, like community peace, does not require that each man love his neighbor – it requires only that they live together in mutual tolerance." He also spoke in his Civil Rights address of the need for eliminating discrimination based on race, and said that "Now the time has come for this Nation to fulfill its promise."

But those messages were not heard or felt by all. In November 1963, Kennedy was killed by an assassin's bullet as he was campaigning for re-election in Dallas, Texas. The entire country was silenced in grief, and the sounds of the horse-drawn caissons in the funeral march in Washington still echo around the world.

The monument itself is a graceful, impressive curved granite and fieldstone arc, with a central medallion showing President Kennedy; well-maintained rose gardens and lawns add to the location. The water fountain and expansive views of the sea, the sun, and the sky remind us of the forward thinking Kennedy, of the difficult times, of the paths started, of the paths not finished, and of the many changes since those times. It is a peaceful place to relax, to feel a connection with time, and to think back, to remember what was. Interpreters in season can answer your questions as well. A small beach is accessible here, too, and it makes a great place to stroll or enjoy the water, much as Kennedy himself had done.

To the right of the monument area are two other locations to see. First, there is the Korean War Memorial. The statue there was erected in 2000, 50 years after the start of the

Korean War. The bronze 8-foot high statue, atop a 3-foot pedestal, was modeled after a photograph that had been taken of Jack Allen of Pennsylvania during his service in Suwon, Korea, in 1951. The photograph itself was taken by Don Duquette, a local resident, as an assignment as a military photographer; the statue was cast in bronze by the sculptor Robert Schure. The statue towers over us and captures the strength and spirit of Allen, and shows his determination as he climbed a ridge near the current border between North and South Korea. Allen had received a Bronze Star for his heroism in 1951; in later years he had studied theater and performed in several plays in New York City. He died in Florida in 1985. The monument itself is dedicated to the thousands of soldiers that died in Korea, missing or killed in action. It is too easy to pass by this monument without reflection, as it looks out over the water and hides in the shadows of the Kennedy Memorial, but it is well worth some time to check it out as well.

To the left of the Korean War Memorial is a great place to relax after the beach, Veterans' Park. Here there are grills, picnic tables, and a shady, relaxing spot to view the water. This is a perfect place for an evening picnic and then a stroll along the beach or to the Harbor. There is a snack bar, a restroom

 and bathhouse, and a small playground as well as access to Veterans' Beach, which boasts calm, warm waters with a stunning view of Lewis Bay and Hyannis Harbor; there are always boats coming and going to be watching. The Nantucket ferries and other boats can easily be seen from here. This park, along with two adjacent monuments, are too easy to simply drive by, but really should not to be missed.

Directions: From Exit 7 on Route 6, go south on Willow Street. At the lights on Route 28, go straight across Route 28 about 0.2 miles further to Main Street, turning right to enter the Main Street area. From Route 28 in West Yarmouth, bear to the left onto Main Street, about 0.2 miles after the Mill Pond area in West Yarmouth. Turn left on Ocean Street and continue 0.4 miles past the Harbor on the left to the Parking for the Kennedy Memorial. The Veterans' Park parking area is 0.1 mile further.

Google Map QR Code:

Hyannis Youth and Community Center

The 105,000 square foot Hyannis Youth and Community Center is a recently constructed recreation facility, open to residents and to the public. Owned by the town of Barnstable, the facility opened in 2009 to replace the old "Kennedy Rink" that had been there for decades. The new Center provides state-of-the-art facilities to support numerous activities for local residents and visitors as well. The facility includes a 12,500 square foot gym that can be used as two full basketball or volleyball courts, two NHL-size skating rinks, function rooms, and a three-lane walking track. The entire facility is easily accessible, with plenty of parking.

There are many different activities available at the Center. Residents pay a lower fee than non-residents, but all are welcome. Daily or yearly membership fees are available, and family fees are available as well. Ice time, gym time, or meeting rooms can be rented for birthday parties, meetings, or special events, as well.

The three-lane elevated walking track is open most days and open to those over 13 years of age. Game rooms with ping pong, pool tables, air hockey and foosball are available at scheduled times each day. There is also a computer lab with multiple computers for use and wi-fi is available. The open gym times can be used for basketball, volleyball, yoga programs nearly every day, and more. There are dedicated adult times and youth times for the use of the facilities.

The Barnstable Recreation Department also runs programs at the Center through the year that include pickleball, yoga, toddler and playgroup activities, stroller skating, skating clinics and classes for all ages and abilities. Public skating is available year round, and is a real change in pace on a hot summer day; skates are available for rent as well. Public skating times and times and dates of all programs can be obtained at the office at the Center entrance, or at an easy-to-use calendar online at the Hyannis Youth and Community Center website. A cafe is available to provide food service on site.

For those interested in seeing hockey games or figure skating, the Center is the home rink for the Barnstable High School Red Raiders boys' and girls' hockey teams as well as the Barnstable Youth Hockey teams. It also has hosted many local and national hockey and figure skating competitions. All of the games and competitions are open to the public.

The Center boasts green technology that includes low-wattage lighting, computer-controlled air systems and motion sensing to control lighting. Solar electric panels on the south roof provide a portion of the Center's electricity use. The $25.6 million project was funded by the State of Massachusetts, the US Department of Education, private fundraising, and the Town of Barnstable.

On a hot day, or on a rainy day, the Hyannis Youth and Community Center may be just what you and your family are looking for.

Directions: From Exit 7 on Route 6, go south on Willow Street. At the lights on Route 28, turn right onto Route 28. At the Airport Rotary, take Route 28 west. 0.3 miles past the Cape Cod Mall, turn left onto Bearse's Way, and follow this 0.8 miles to the Hyannis Youth Center on the right, at the small rotary.

Google Map QR Code:

The Cape Cod Mall

The Cape Cod Mall is a key destination on a rainy summer day as it is the only enclosed regional mall in the area; there are lots of things to do here, and plenty of parking year round.

Large anchor stores at the Cape Cod Mall include Target, Macys, Barnes and Noble bookstore, Marshall's, and Best Buy. There are dozens of other stores, too, including GNC, Children's Place, Sephora, Olympia Sports, Sunglass Hut, Payless Shoes, Aeropostale, Hollister, Newbury Comics, Talbot's, Loft, American Eagle, Bath and Body Works, Victoria's Secret, several jewelry stores, and many more. There are also several hair and nail salons.

Barnes and Noble bookstore is a great and popular place to browse on a rainy day, with comfortable chairs in the upper level and a Starbuck's cafe on the lower level. A great stop for children is the carousel at the Food Court end of the mall, always a favorite with children. There are also several small rides for children in the main hallway of the Mall, as well as a toy store. The TenPin Eatery provides a restaurant, bowling lanes, a virtual reality area, laser tag and a game room. If you are looking for even more variety in stores, a short drive south on Route 132 is the Christmas Tree Shop, famous for its bargains, and in that same complex is a grocery store, candy store, and candle store; additional stores are found across Route 132.

There is a free wi-fi service at the Mall, so you can just connect to it with your smartphone, tablet, or laptop. There is also enhanced cellular reception inside the building, to improve your cell signal inside. In addition, there is a Simon Malls Mobile app that can be downloaded from Apple or Google to allow you to see special events, sales, gift card balances, and a map of the mall.

There is plenty of seating around the mall for those more inclined to wait and watch while others shop! A popular resting spot in the Mall is the 400-seat International Food Court. While Coca Cola machines are available throughout the Mall, you can buy all sorts of foods and beverages at the Food Court. There is a wide range of food from Thai to Japanese, to pizza, to subs or ice cream. There are also several restaurants, a pretzel shop, frozen yogurt and a donut shop in other locations in the mall.

There are also charging stations with seating for charging phones or tablets. An ATM machine is located near the food court. Restroom facilities and a family restroom facility are located near the food court as well. Baby changing stations are available in the Family Room, found near the food court. You can also rent a stroller at the food court area. You can check a coat or packages with Guest Services, near the J. Crew store. Guest Services can also provide wheelchairs upon request.

At the Target end of the mall, you can gain access to Regal Cinemas with 12 screens, a busy but fun stop on a rainy summer day. There is plenty of parking just outside the Cinema, on the south side of the Mall, as well. Maybe the sun will be shining outside after the movie!

While most people drive to the Mall, there is bus service (Sea Line) that stops at the Food Court entrance to the Mall; this bus can take you to Main Street in Hyannis, the bus and train station in Hyannis, and to the County complex on Route 6A in Barnstable.

The Cape Cod Mall is a Simon Properties mall. Simon Properties, located in Indianapolis, Indiana, owns over 325 different commercial properties across the United States, South America, and Asia, and employs over 5,500 individuals.

Directions: To reach the Cape Cod Mall, take Route 6 to Exit 6. Take Route 132 south and proceed straight on Route 132, 2.6 miles to the Mall on the right. Parking is found in front of the Mall, behind the Mall, and to the right of the Mall.

Google Map QR Code:

Cape Cod Potato Chips Factory Tour

The factory for Cape Cod Potato Chips is right in Hyannis and readily accessible with excellent parking for free tours of the plant. A bonus is the free potato chips that you can get at the end of the free self-guided tour! You can visit the plant during regular business hours on weekdays, but not on weekends. Once you have parked, just follow the seagull prints to the tour start! This is a fun thing to do if you have a half hour or so in the area – nearly a quarter million people visit the plant every year!

The tour shows you all of the steps in the manufacture of these world-renowned potato chips, from the harvesting of the potatoes in farms across the nation, to the "spudnick" machine that brings the potatoes into the plant, then to the mechanical slicing, and finally to the cooking in large kettles of pure canola oil. After cooking, the chips are spun and drained and then seasoned. Finally, they are weighed and bagged, and then prepared for shipping to destinations all over the U.S. While you cannot enter the food preparation area itself due to health regulations, you can see all the steps of the production in the factory through the large glass windows along the tour. Large wall displays explain the processes that you will be seeing. This is a short tour that, depending on how long you linger, may take a half hour or so. It is great for children to see how a food product is manufactured from beginning to end. Photographs are not allowed during the tour. After the tour, you can sample the chips, and also can visit the gift store where you can buy T shirts, sweatshirts, hats, mugs, tote bags, cook books, puzzles, and children's books.

The Cape Cod Potato Chip logo includes a picture of the dunes of Cape Cod, with the ocean in the background; the lighthouse is Nauset Lighthouse that you can see in Eastham. The lighthouse was first built in Chatham in 1877, and then moved to Eastham in 1923. It has been moved back from the ocean several times since then, due to heavy erosion in the area. All of the Cape Cod Potato Chip products show the lighthouse image. At the gifts store, you can also buy dozens of different types of chips and popcorn, either by the bag or by the box. The tour is a great rainy day activity, or something to do before or after the beach; the plant is just a short drive from the Cape Cod Mall or Main Street in Hyannis, so maybe it is a great place to visit before or after shopping or dining as well. The tour is a popular destination, so be prepared for crowds, depending on the time of the day.

Cape Cod Potato chips got its start during the 1980's in a

small natural foods store started by Lynn Bernard on Main Street in Hyannis. Steve Bernard started the company on a very small budget, making the chips in a kettle in the store, and selling chips right in the same store, about 200 bags a day initially, using potatoes from a farm in Rhode Island. Even now, the chips are cooked in kettles and stirred by hand, which is a little different in approach to the conveyer belt cooking that is used to make most chips. No additives are used to make the chips. The result is thicker, crisper chips that some consider to be gourmet chips. By the mid 1980's, the chips were widely available and in great demand. In 1985, the company was purchased by Anheuser Busch, then repurchased by Bernard in 1996, and then sold again to Lance Corporation in 1999. Currently, Cape Cod Potato chips is owned by the Snyders-Lance Corporation, centered in Charlotte, N.C. The company owns more than a dozen snack manufacturers in nine different states.

Directions: From Route 6, take exit 6 to Route 132 toward Hyannis. Turn left at the 6th light onto Independence Drive. Follow that straight for about 1 mile, and take your second right onto Breed's Hill Road. Cape Cod Potato Chips is on Breed's Hill Road, on your left. Once you are on Independence Drive, keep your windows open, the smell of those chips will let you know that you are close!

Google Map QR Code:

ABOUT QR CODES

QR stands for Quick Response. QR codes are similar to bar codes and were first used in 1994 in automobile manufacturing to keep track of parts for the vehicle. Now, they are used extensively for many purposes, including providing quick access to web pages.

In our book, each QR code brings you to a custom Google Map which will show you the exact location that you are looking for, as well as the other roads in the area, and where to park. The only information in the QR code is the web address of the map, nothing else; there is no tracking at all of the use of the code. The QR code simply saves having to type in a lengthy address to find the map.

You can just use your cell phone to view the QR code, and then the map will be opened quickly and easily on your phone. Once the map opens, you can zoom in to see area roads in detail; you can switch from street map view to satellite view and zoom in on the location.

If you click on a star in the map view, it will use the star as your destination and you can then use Google Maps to guide you automatically that location using your cell phone as a free GPS. This is amazing technology, linking the printed book with our cellphones! If you prefer, our book also has written directions for each location as well, including exactly how to get to each spot in the book and where to park.

Many phones now have QR code reading already built in to the camera. If your phone does not have a QR code reader already installed, you can find many apps that will read QR codes either in the Google Store or on Apple; just search for "QR Code." You also need to have the Google Maps app installed, as well as the Chrome app. Your location must be allowed in the app permission settings for both Chrome and Google maps.

ABOUT THE AUTHOR

William E. Peace holds both Bachelor's and Master's degrees from Tufts University and has taught science on Cape Cod since 1973 at both the secondary and undergraduate levels. An avid nature enthusiast and bicyclist, he has lived on Cape Cod for over forty years and knows the area as only a local resident could. He has also led walks at Sandy Neck Barrier Beach, and worked as a research associate at the Cape Cod National Seashore.

The author of several books and webpages, Bill has three grown children. Besides his family, Bill is interested in photography, camping and the outdoors, computers and education, and gardening.

Bill's books include *The Cape Cod Bike Book* which was first published in 1984 and is still the go-to guide on Cape bicycling, authored by a local Cape Cod resident, and published and revised annually. He also has published a new series of *Cape Cod Visitor's Guides: Free and Inexpensive Things to Do* on the Cape, with books about the Upper Cape, Mid Cape, Lower Cape, and Outer Cape.

Each book gives a real insider's view to the Cape, information about points of interest, notes on history, ecology, where to stop, what to see, and some things that you might otherwise miss along the way. Bill loves Cape Cod, and he wants you to love it too, and he shares that passion in all the work that he does.

For more information about things to see on Cape Cod, check out Bill's main webpage, at *williampeacecapecod.com* The page has links to his other pages about bicycling on the Cape, lighthouses on Cape Cod, windmills on Cape Cod, walks and hikes on Cape Cod, playgrounds on Cape Cod, and things to do on rainy days on Cape Cod.

PHOTOGRAPHS

Dennis

Scargo Hill Tower: Scargo Tower (p. 5), Scargo Lake (p. 6)

Hokum Rock: Hokum Rock Ledges (p. 8), Hokum Rock Conservation Lands (p. 9)

Nobscusset Conservation Area: South Peninsula Trail (p. 11), Nickerson Point Trail (p. 12), Nobscusset Burial Ground Marker (p. 13), South Peninsula Trail (p. 13)

Johnny Kelley Recreation Area: Recreation Area Sign (p. 15), Braille Trail/Walking Trail (p. 16), Johnny Kelley Play Area (p. 17)

North Side Beaches: Mayflower Beach Dunes (p. 18), Mayflower Beach Sandflats (p. 19), Mayflower Beach Beachgrass (p. 20),

Bass River Park: Looking Toward Highbank Road (p. 22), Looking Toward South Yarmouth (p. 23)

Playgrounds in the Mid-Cape: Community Building Playground (p. 26), Mike Stacey Playground (p. 27), Luke's Love Playground (p. 28)

Main Street, Dennis Port: Mural in Dennis Port (p. 30), Visitor's Park in Dennis Port (p. 31), Main Street Dennis Port (p. 32), Dennis Public Library (p. 33)

Yarmouth

Bass Hole Boardwalk: Boardwalk with Sandy Neck in Background (p. 35), View from Accessible Boardwalk (p. 36), Gray's Beach (p. 37)

Yarmouth Botanic Trails: Yarmouth Port Historic Area Sign (p. 39), Botanic Trail gravel pathway (p. 40), Kelley Chapel (p. 41), Yarmouth Historic Society Building (p. 43)

Captains' Mile and More: Captain Bangs Hallet House (p. 45), Captain's Home Plaque (p. 45), National Register of Historic Places Plaque (p. 46), Winslow Crocker House (p. 47), Hallet's Store (p. 48)

Peter G. Homer Recreation Area: Homer Recreation Area Playground (p. 49), Picnic Area Near Homer Playground (p. 50), Homer Area Facilities Building (p. 50), Yarmouth Bike Path (p. 51), Bocce Courts at Homer Area (p. 52)

Flax Pond Recreation Area: Town of Yarmouth Recreation Sign (p. 53), Lorusso Lodge (p. 54), Flax Pond Picnic Area (p. 55), Flax Pond Summer Program Mural (p. 56)

Judah Baker Windmill: Judah Baker Windmill (p. 57), Windmill Restoration Plaque (p. 58), Baker Windmill Tailpiece (p. 59)

Veterans' Park, Yarmouth: Veterans' Park (p. 61), Veteran's Park (p. 62), Veterans' Park View of Bass River (p. 62), Jolly Captain Lighthouse (p. 63)

Wilbur Park: Wilbur Park View of Bass River (p. 64)

Hyannis

Main Street, Hyannis: Federated Church of Hyannis (p. 66), Main Street Shoppes (p. 67), West End of Main Street (p. 68)

Kennedy Legacy Trail and Museum: Kennedy Museum (p.70), What Could Have Been Statue (p. 72), Peace Corps Recognition on Legacy Trail (p. 73)

Hyannis Harbor: Nantucket Ferry (p. 74), Fishing Piers (pp. 75-76), Baxter's Wharf (p. 77)

Kennedy Memorial: John F. Kennedy Memorial Sign (p. 78), Presidential Seal (p. 79), Kennedy Medallion (p. 80)

Veterans' Park, Hyannis: Korean War Memorial (p. 81), Veterans' Park Picnic Grove (p. 82)

Hyannis Youth and Community Center: Community Center Building (p. 85)

Cape Cod Mall: Cape Cod Mall Entrance (p.87), Carousel at Cape Cod Mall (p. 88), Cape Cod Mall Food Court Entrance (p. 89)

Cape Cod Potato Chip Factory Tour: Factory Tour Sign (p. 91)

INDEX

Dennis

Yarmouth

Hyannis

Notes

Made in the USA
Middletown, DE
28 January 2020

83861879R00060